Mindfulness, Self-Love, and Meditation for Teens

Guided Meditations and Highly Effective Techniques to Empower Teens with Self-Confidence, Beat Anxiety, and Improve Mental Health

Amora K. Rose

James Sharma

professional before attempting any techniques outlined in this book.

By reading this document, the reader agrees that under no circumstances is the author responsible for any losses, direct or indirect, that are incurred as a result of the use of the information contained within this document, including, but not limited to, errors, omissions, or inaccuracies.

Table of Contents

Your Free Gift!

Hey there! I just wanted to express my gratitude for buying my book. As a token of appreciation, I would love to offer you my books and a Guided Meditation Audio completely for FREE!

It's my way of saying thank you for your support, and I truly hope it helps you in your journey toward managing anxiety.

 To Download The Guided Meditation Audio Scan The QR Code Or Go To: obiez.com/meditationaudio

Anxiety Relief Guide

- How Anxiety Creeps Up and How to avoid it
- 4 Practical Tools to Empowering yourself to handle your Emotions
- A Simple but Extremely Effective Technique to Treat Panic Attacks
- Little known Secret to Be Socially Fearless
- And Much More

 To Download The Book Scan The QR Code or Go To: obiez.com/anxiety

The Power² Of Gratitude For Teens

- The Secret To Gratitude in Teens
- 5 Ways Gratitude Can Exponentiate a Teens Life
- How a Simple Action Can Improve Your Family's Relationship
- And Much More

 To Download The Book Scan The QR Code or Go To: obiez.com/gratitude

Introduction

"Meditation practice isn't about trying to throw ourselves away and become something better. It's about befriending who we are already" — Pema Chodron

Dear Diary,

Everyone around me seems to have everything together. My classmates talk about which universities they're going to apply to, where they'll travel to after high school or which jobs they will try to get. I don't know what I want to do. I think it's crazy that I'm 16, and people expect me to know what I'll do with the rest of my life.

Why do people have this idea that they have to do one thing anyway? What if I want to be a teacher for a few years and then switch to being a painter or an entrepreneur? Why does it seem like I have all of these huge choices to make, but no idea which path to take? Why do all of my friends know, but I don't?

Other people in my grade have boyfriends, girlfriends, or

partners. I have a best friend, but I've never been in love before. I play volleyball and do CrossFit. I am not the best, but I'm not the worst either. I am just wandering through life, unsure and stumbling.

I wish there were some magic button to press to ignite my brain to tell me what to do and which path to take. Anything to just give me a hint at who I am and what I'm meant to do. I worry all the time about what I wear, how I look, what I say, how I react. I worry about everything, but no one notices. All they see is the shell I walk around in.

Love, Me.

* * * *

The above diary entry is not unlike that of many teens. Feeling unsure, worried about what others think, and anxious about the future. Some experience bullying and isolation at school or at home. The constant information, jam-packed schedules, maintaining healthy relationships, navigating the visible and invisible changes within the body are overwhelming, to say the least. Inviting mindfulness and meditation will bring calm and peace into your life, thereby reducing stress and pain, as well as feelings of anxiety or depression. By practicing self-love in the form of meditation, you will increase self-compassion and give yourself more grace as you move through this life (Creswell &

9

Khoury, 2019).

When you begin to train the attention of the mind, you can observe your feelings instead of being absorbed by them. While mindfulness, self-love and meditation may be buzz words you've heard thrown around, they are amazing, free, accessible tools that can help you to find your power, grow into who you are, live a life that reflects your true self, your beliefs and your values. Through meditation, mindfulness, and self-love practices, you will gain compassion and empathy for yourself and others, you will be able to treat yourself with kindness, and you may feel less alone knowing that no one is free of life's challenges (Moore, 2022).

Before getting started, it's important that you know what we're talking about here. Mindfulness is quality, and meditation is a practice. To be mindful is to be aware of your surroundings and yourself. To live on purpose rather than on autopilot. Meditation is a practice. Meditation means to do nothing, to slow down, to stop. To allow your thoughts to come and go without reacting to, judging, or dissecting them. Meditation is something that requires stillness of mind and body; to become an observer of your inner world (Schultz, 2020).

This book is a tool that you can revisit for practices that offer self-love and kindness, calming mind and body through connection and awareness, practices to help you live with more compassion, love and confidence.

If I'm being honest, no one really knows what they're doing at any age. People look like they have it all together on the outside, but inside, their mind worries questions and feels just like yours. The goal is to become aware of our thoughts, how we speak to, how to lean into love and give ourselves and others more love and compassion.

Continue through this book and dive into yourself through numerous mindfulness and self-love meditations created just for you.

Chapter 1: The Basics

"Mindfulness is a way of befriending ourselves and our experience" —Jon Kabat-Zinn

The goal of Mindfulness, Self-love, and Meditation is to help you cultivate feelings of love and kindness for yourself. To help you bring all the love you gave, in ways that enable you to develop self-confidence when faced with challenges. Oftentimes, people speak to and about themselves in a way they would never even consider speaking to or about others. This type of meditation will help you gain awareness of your inner dialogue and give you the space to change your narrative (Nunez, 2020).

Meditation is like training your attention. It may sound easy, the idea of sitting still, doing nothing and maybe not saying anything, but I assure you it is a life-long practice. Meditation's goal is for you to achieve an emotionally calm and stable state. Mindfulness is the quality of being aware (Creswell & Khoury, 2019; Schultz, 2020).

The goal of meditation is not to empty your mind, but rather to control your attention. Instead of following every thought that comes into your mind, you notice it and watch it pass by like a cloud through the sky. You don't judge it, hold onto it or react to it. Simply notice. Breathe and notice (Creswell & Khoury, 2019).

Before diving into Mindfulness, Self-love, and Meditation, let's start by practicing two meditations; one that encourages awareness of thought and the other to develop mindful awareness. This is an act of self-love. To build more love for yourself, you can act in ways that support your mental and physical growth, which will help bring you to a state of appreciation for yourself. All you need is a comfortable place to sit where you won't be disturbed for a few minutes. The first practice aims to make you aware of your thoughts and gives you a strategy to refocus on the moment as opposed to following thoughts that pop up. A sort-of building block for introducing the meditative practice. The goal is not to have no thought, but to train the mind, not to follow each thought. To become an observer of the self (Creswell & Khoury, 2019; Schultz, 2020).

Meditation: Thought Seeker (Two minutes) (Amir-Yaffe, 2021)

If you have a phone or a timer, set it now for two minutes. I like to set mine to chime, but you choose whichever calming sound you like.

Settle into a comfortable seated position.

Breathe.

Bring your attention to the connection between your bottom and the floor.

Notice the weight of your body, grounding you in place.

Breathe.

Now, bring your attention to the breath.

Take one deep inhale and follow your breath as far as you can.

Notice the slight pause between the switch to exhale.

Exhale deeply. Following the exhale as far as you can.

Repeat three times.

Inhale fully through the nose.

Exhale completely through the mouth.

Resume your natural rhythm of the breath.

Now, I invite you to count to 10.

Each time a thought pops into your mind, begin counting again starting from 1.

Repeat this practice of counting and re-starting for the remainder of this practice.

When your timer chimes, take one more focused inhale and exhale before opening your eyes.

Prompts for Reflection

In a personal journal, or simply reflecting in your mind, ask yourself the following questions:

What was the quality of my thoughts? Were they positive or negative or a mix of both?

_____

_____

_____

_____

_____

_____

_____

What has happened today that might be influencing my thoughts?

_____

_____

_____

_____

_____

How did I feel before, during and after this practice?

_____

_____

_____

_____

_____

A step toward building more self-appreciation is to become aware of your thoughts, their quality, quantity and focus. This awareness enables you to gain more self-love, and control over impulses and build open-mindedness to your actions and perspectives.

Mindfulness: Eating (Four minutes)

As human beings, our minds are constantly thinking, moving and working. Even as we sleep our subconscious mind is at work. To be mindful means to be aware of yourself, and of your surroundings. A way of paying attention is through the use of the five senses. One way to practice this is through mindful eating. This helps you get in tune with your senses and to pay attention to the present moment by inviting visualization techniques. Though this practice is food focused, the ability to use your senses to understand the world around you helps create a deeper understanding of yourself (Robledo, 2021).

Eating and nourishing your body is an act of self-love, so let's begin by choosing a piece of fruit or chocolate or something yummy, but do not start eating right away. Begin by placing the food in front of you and simply observe it.

Notice the shape, color and texture of the food you're looking at.

Ask yourself, how did it get here? Did it grow on a tree? What process did this food take to get from where it grew to your table?

If you chose an orange, try to picture the seed of the tree being planted. Imagine yourself digging in the dirt with your fingers, cool and crumbly. Imagine yourself placing the tiny seed into the ground and covering it gently with the earth.

Listen to the rain as it waters the seed, helping to grow into a fully formed orange tree full of beautiful bright oranges and vibrant green leaves.

Picture someone picking the orange, placing it in a crate, and shipping it to the store in which you or your parents bought it.

Visualize yourself or your parents buying the food you're looking at and bringing it home to set on the counter.

Now, pick up your food. Hold it gently in your hands. Notice the weight and temperature. Is it light, soft, heavy, or hard? Is it bumpy or smooth? Big or little? Warm, hot, room temperature, or cool?

Now that you have visualized the process of farm-to-table, offer gratitude for the process and the people who have made it possible for you to eat this.

Next, smell your snack. Can you smell anything? Is it sweet or sour? Fragrant or smelly? Spicy or savory?

Take a bite, but do not swallow immediately. Pay attention to the sound it makes as you break it between your teeth.

Notice the flavor and the feel of it moving around your mouth.

Finish eating your snack without any distractions. No screens, no talking, nothing besides you and your snack. Enjoy!

Prompts for Reflection

In a personal journal, or simply reflecting in your mind, ask yourself the following questions:

What thoughts did I have before, during and after this process?

_____

_____

_____

_____

_____

_____

How does this food make you feel?

_____

_____

_____

_____

_____

_____

Do you notice any difference in your mood or your body from before eating until now, after eating?

_____

_____

_____

_____

_____

How did it feel tuning into your senses and eating mindfully?

_____

_____

_____

_____

_____

* * * *

The purpose of this first chapter is to help you understand what Mindfulness, Self-love, and Meditation are. As we go through to the next chapter, we will hone in on creating self-love, compassion, and kindness. Hold on to the notion that meditation is to steady the mind, to exercise the muscle of attention, and mindfulness is the quality of attention we seek. We seek to be present, to be conscious, to be thoughtful. It is through the practice of mindfulness and meditation that we gain more insight into ourselves, enabling us to develop self-confidence and compassion for ourselves and others (Schultz, 2020).

Chapter 2: How to Improve Your Quality of Life

When we are mindful, we take in what is happening and are more able to choose how we react. In practicing mindful self-love meditation regularly, you increase your mind's ability to respond consciously instead of reacting impulsively. When our minds are still or steady, we can see a situation for what it is; we can offer ourselves love and compassion. When our minds are reactive and following impulsive thoughts, we can only see a situation from our perspective (Creswell & Khoury, 2019).

Have you ever had a hard morning and just snapped at someone who hadn't been part of the reason for the hard morning? For example, you didn't sleep well, your sibling took forever in the bathroom in the morning, leaving you no time to get ready, you didn't have time to eat breakfast, got to school late, your teacher gave a pop quiz, and then your friend asked you to share your notes because they didn't take any and you felt instantly annoyed, rolled your eyes and threw your notes at them? Your friend, likely confused and upset, asked what's wrong, and you just groaned and looked at the papers in front of you?

This is an impulsive reaction based on your emotions and the quality of your morning leading up to this moment. While the person who practices mindfulness may also be annoyed and grumpy after a morning like that, they are more likely to access other parts of the mind, able to see other perspectives; like the part of the mind that knew your friend wasn't at school the previous day and just needed some help. This is, as Tich Nhat Hanh says, to see reality as it is: you had a hard morning, making you feel grumpy, and your friend feels nervous about the test and needs help because they missed a day of school. When we are mindful and compassionate, we can choose to respond in a more appropriate manner for the situations we face (Creswell & Khoury, 2019; Selva, 2017).

The self-love-focused meditation is one that you can practice in order to develop more compassion and understanding of the self and others. It helps ground you in the present and trains the mind to offer self-love and compassion rather than criticism and judgement. According to Moore (2022), it incorporates the following views and benefits:

- Self-kindness

Speaking kindly to and about yourself, even when going through challenging times, even if the hard time is your fault. Cultivating unconditional love for self.

- Common Humanity

Learning that everyone in the world experiences difficult periods in their lives, uncomfortable emotions, makes mistakes, faces challenges and worries. It is the universal human experience and realizing this can help grow empathy, compassion and kindness.

- Mindfulness

Personal awareness of negative thoughts and difficult feelings. Not beating yourself up for having these thoughts, just noticing their presence and accepting the moments for what they are.

- Good Mental Health

We all have mental health, but the quality and state of our mental health varies throughout our lives, impacted by various circumstances, events and experiences. Practicing mindful self-love meditation can boost the quality of your mental health.

- Optimism

Research shows that people who practice meditation are more optimistic or positive about life. They have an increased ability to see the good side of things and to seek solutions rather than problems.

- Builds Resilience

Meditation practice is often recommended to those suffering from anxiety and depression, as it helps to build resilience to combat the overwhelming doom that comes along with these illnesses. This increased resilience is also linked to processing pain more easily as you have more control over the mind.

* * * *

Now that you understand the basics and benefits of Mindfulness, Self-love, and meditation, continue on to Chapter 3 where you will find suggestions for incorporating this into your daily or weekly routine.

Chapter 3: Making your Dream Routine

"When we get too caught up in the busyness of the world, we lose connection with one another and ourselves" —Jack Kornfield

With friends and family obligations, school and extracurricular activities, relationships, jobs, and so much more it can feel overwhelming to try to add something else to your already jam-packed life. The best part about meditation is that you can dedicate as much or as little time as you want. Even just two minutes each day is enough to jumpstart your brain to gain more awareness, and you will begin to notice yourself tuning into your mind and emotions more frequently than before meditating (Gelles, 2019).

According to Gelles (2019), the two main steps you can take to help add mindful self-love meditation into your day are to:

- Pick a time

Because meditation requires nothing besides yourself, anytime of day is fine, but many people report that adding a few minutes to the morning or prior to going to bed is the easiest routine to keep up. Pick whatever time will work best for you and stick to it. The key to making time for a routine is to do it over and over again at the same time, much like brushing your teeth. In fact, it's not impossible to meditate while you brush your teeth.

- Choose a spot

You are committing to stillness, so choose a spot in which you are unlikely to be disturbed. Once you develop a decent practice, it may even be possible to meditate amongst chaos like in the kitchen of your family home. However, until then, it's best to find somewhere peaceful and comfortable where you feel safe and at ease when closing your eyes.

* * * *

That is it. Pick a time, choose a spot and stick to it! While there are props like cushions or stools, they are not necessary to begin a practice, but they can make you more comfortable. Rather than purchasing these items, a pillow from the couch or your bed can do the same placed under your sit bones to elevate your hips a bit making you more comfortable. You do not need to cross your legs if it is uncomfortable for you, you can sit on your bottom, your knees, lay down. You can be on a chair, on the floor, or even on your bed. You could even practice in the car or on the bus on your way to school. Just be still, focus on your breathing, and be here now (Gelles, 2019).

Some people find being still extremely difficult and in these cases, you could choose to incorporate meditation into movement. For example, yoga connects the breath and the movement creating one steady flow encouraging the mind to focus on the present rather than whatever happened in the past or worrying about what comes next. There are also walking meditations that you could practice in nature or simply walking down the street or the halls at school or like the sample in Chapter 1, mindful eating. So many ways to tune into your body, your mind and your emotions. No matter your path, walk it with love and honor your needs (Gelles, 2019).

Oftentimes when trying something new or building a routine, you will notice a rise in self-criticism, wondering why you can't just shut your mind off and be still. Everyone has this. The mind cannot be shut off but you can train your attention. Meditation is not a sport, not a competition, not a goal to be achieved. It is a practice to invite self-kindness and compassion into your life. Some people feel sleepy after meditating, but that's totally normal. If this is the case, do your practice in the evening after all of your activities for the day have finished. Others feel pain or uncomfortable sensations when trying to sit in the traditional pose with folded legs; if this is you, then change your position (Gelles, 2019)!

The key is to want to improve, to manage to let go of your expectations knowing that this is not a practice that can be perfected. Simply go forward knowing that meditation can reduce stress, build resilience, and create a calm and peaceful existence. Continue on to Chapter 4 where you will find three guided meditations to practice at your leisure.

Chapter 4: Meditations for Happiness, Gratitude, and Love

"You are the sky. Everything else is just the weather" —*Pema Chodron*

Before diving into the meditations below, take a moment to reflect on the above quote and record your thoughts here or in a personal journal.

_____

_____

_____

_____

_____

_____

Mindfulness, Self-Love, and Meditation is to observe your thoughts without judgement while offering yourself compassion. Watch your thoughts pass by as if they are the clouds and you are the sky. They are there, they may change your color or the way you look, but the sky is always there, just like you. While two minutes is fine for beginning and developing a routine, the longer you meditate, the more benefits you will receive. The meditations below have suggested times and can be lengthened or shortened by sitting longer and following the breath, observing your thoughts, or repeating an affirmation, or by ending early, ensuring that you take a deep inhale and exhale before moving on (Moore, 2022).

For each of the following meditations, choose a chime or sound that is peaceful for you, and set it to sound before and after the meditation, or use a personal bell or bowl to commence and complete the practice. It is a nice way to trigger the mind into a relaxed state, but not necessary if it is not your preference.

Meditation: Fostering Joy (Three Minutes)

Find yourself a quiet space to practice and before getting comfortable, wiggle your body a bit.

Shake your arms, letting go of any tension you are holding.

Wiggle your fingers and toes.

Do small circles with your ankles.

Move your hips from side to side.

Now, settle in. Sit in a position that comes with little effort for you.

Roll your shoulders up and back, encouraging a tall spine.

Rest your arms at your sides or your hands gently on your thighs.

Fix your gaze in front of you or close your eyes.

Bring your attention to the connection between your body and the earth.

Inhale softly through the nose.

Exhale gently through the mouth.

As you breathe, hold your attention on the connection between you and the floor.

Notice the slight pressing feeling, the temperature, the texture against your body.

Feel the energy you receive from this connection.

You are supported, you are awake, you are sitting tall, you are alive.

Gently bring your attention to the breath.

Notice the rise and fall of the body as breath runs through freely, giving life to you.

Aware of the effortless connection between the body and breath. No resistance, just acceptance.

The breath and body flow as one.

Feel your body soften as you continue to breathe.

Be curious about the wonder that is life within your body.

Slowly shift your attention to your heart.

Place your right hand over your heart for a moment and feel the beat of life within you.

Hold your hand here, connecting with the beating heart for three breaths.

Inhale softly through the nose.

Exhale gently through the mouth.

Feel your body soften and release your hand back down to your side or thigh.

Bring your attention up to your face.

Relax the muscles in your face, your shoulders, your belly, your legs, and your feet.

Breathe.

Direct your attention to your mouth and your lips.

Pull the corners of your lips up slightly and notice the feeling this gives you.

Notice where your mind goes or how the body feels at the beginning of a smile and hold onto this joy.

Place one hand over your belly and the other over your heart.

Feel the connection between your hands and your body.

Inhale fully.

Exhale completely.

Smile.

-Inspired by Fargo (2020).

* * * *

In a personal journal or here in the pages of this book, I invite you to write. Write whatever is on your mind. You could put pen to paper and write as if mind and pen are one. You could make a list of emotions that arose throughout the practice, you could doodle while reflecting on this meditation.

_____

_____

_____

_____

_____

Describe the feeling of smiling on purpose from beginning to end. From lifting the corners of the mouth, joy stretching across your face, holding that softly, and taking a deep sighs before relaxing the muscles.

_____

_____

_____

_____

_____

_____

Smile every day. Train your attention to notice when you smile. Be conscious of who is around, what you're doing and where you are. Notice the feelings in your mind and body. Smile on your dark days when all you want to do is hide away. Smile when you feel joy and smile when everything hurts. Self-love is meant to be unconditional.

Meditation: Gratitude (Five Minutes)

Get into a comfortable position, whatever that looks like for you.

Breathe.

Settle into this practice, into this moment, into this space.

Ground yourself by bringing your attention to the connection of body and ground.

Inhale through the nose.

Exhale through the mouth.

Relax your arms by your sides or on your legs and, if you feel comfortable, close your eyes, or relax your gaze.

As you breathe, notice any areas of tension. Visualize the areas and breathe into those spaces for relief.

Full inhale through the nose.

Sigh and exhale through the mouth.

Bring your attention to where you feel the most relaxed and calm. It might be your shoulders, your belly, your hips, your face. Wherever you feel at ease.

Inhale fully.

I am grateful for this peace within my body.

Exhale completely.

Be aware of the sensations in your body as you breathe.

Allow your belly to inflate as you inhale and deflate as you exhale.

Gently place your hands on your belly and feel the movement of breath as your belly rises and falls.

Breathe.

Now, gently guide your attention to the sensation of breath through the nose.

Keeping your natural rhythm of breath, follow the inhale and exhale, bringing your attention to the space where the inhale becomes the exhale.

Breathe.

Inhale through the nose.

I am grateful for this awareness of my body.

Gently part your lips and exhale.

Be mindful of the breath within the body as you take one full inhale and one complete exhale.

I am thankful for this time to meditate.

For the next ten natural rhythm breath cycles, try to hold on to this feeling of gratitude.

There is no need to rush, nothing to do, nowhere else to be.

Breathe.

Notice when the mind wanderers.

Acknowledge the thought, watch it float by, and refocus your attention on the breath.

As you breathe, offer thanks to yourself for making this time. Thanks to your body for carrying you through life and allowing you to do so many wonderful things.

The final inhale of the practice. Deep breath in through the nose, feeling the breath fill you with abundance.

I have everything I need.

Complete exhale, allowing the body to soften, offering a sense of peace.

I am grateful to be a part of this beautiful universe.

*Inspired by "Gratitude Meditation Script" (n.d.) and Great Meditation (2021).

* * * *

To increase self-appreciation, I encourage you to begin a gratitude journal. Begin each day and/or end each night by writing at least one thing you are grateful for. This can be something as big as getting to go to your favorite musician's concert or something small like seeing a pretty sunrise on the way to school. The practice of searching for something that makes you thankful can increase your mind control as you are intentionally thinking about something and your love of self. Other benefits of journaling according to Milne (2019) include:

- Developing mindfulness.

- Increasing emotional intelligence and awareness.

- Enhancing memory and academic performance.

- Improving communication skills.

- Boosting creativity and confidence.

- Building resilience and healing through reflection.

I prefer to record my gratitude in a bedside journal using complete sentences, however my best friend prefers to record hers on a notepad in her phone in the form of a list and sometimes emojis. No matter your methods, this practice is beneficial for increasing gratitude and self-love.

Meditation: Love and Kindness (Ten Minutes)

Take a moment to let your body sway while standing.

If you feel comfortable, allow your eyes to close as you softly shift from side to side or in small or big circles.

Allow your arms to wave up and down as you breathe, releasing any tension or worries.

Roll your shoulders forward and backward in a fluid motion, nice and gentle.

When ready, allow yourself to come into a comfortable seated position.

Pull the flesh away from your sit bones, lengthen your spine, and relax your arms with hands turned upward on your thighs.

Breathe.

Settle into this moment, into this space.

Allow your natural rhythm of breath to flow freely as you complete any minor adjustments before coming to a still seated pose.

Imagine your breath flowing and swirling through the body as you inhale and exhale.

Notice any sounds outside of the room.

Without trying to tell yourself a story about these sounds, what they are and where they are coming from, just notice them.

Now, bring your attention to the sounds within the room or space you are seated in.

Breathe.

Allow your breath to flow naturally without trying to control it.

Notice your body as it moves in and out with each cycle.

Placing one hand over your hear and the other over your belly, take one deep inhale and hold for 1, 2, 3, 4.

Completely exhale and hold for 1, 2, 3, 4.

Repeat this practice of inhale-hold-exhale-hold for three counts before resuming the natural breath.

Imagine someone who embodies love and kindness to you. This could be someone you know or a complete stranger. Picture this warm person sitting across from you.

As you breathe, hold on to the feeling this person evokes in you.

With your hands still on your body, bring your attention to your heart.

Without yourself in mind, repeat the following words as you breathe, filling the body with life and exhaling love.

May I be happy.

May I be healthy.

May I be safe.

May I live with ease.

Inhale fully.

Exhale completely.

Coming back to the natural breath, hands remain in place over the belly and heart.

For the next five breath cycles, sit with these words in your mind and notice how the body responds.

May I be happy.

May I be healthy.

May I be safe.

May I live with ease.

Inhale through the nose for 1, 2, 3, 4, 5.

Hold for 1, 2, 3.

Exhale through the mouth for 1, 2, 3, 4, 5.

Now, bring to mind someone close to you. Someone you love and appreciate.

Imagine this person sitting in front of you.

Inhale fully.

Exhale completely.

Allow your mind to wander to the happy memories you share with this person.

Think about the times you have shared.

About the feelings you have when you know you're going to spend time with this person.

How you feel in their presence and in the moments after you part ways.

Send some love and kindness to them by repeating these words:

Inhale.

May you be happy.

Exhale.

Inhale.

May you be healthy.

Exhale.

Inhale.

May you be safe.

Exhale.

Inhale.

May you live with ease.

Exhale.

Allow your breath to even out, bringing your awareness to the connection between your hand and your belly.

Feel your belly rise on the inhale.

And fall on the exhale.

Gently bring your attention up to your heart. Notice the feel of your hand against your chest. Notice the temperature, the light touch.

Inhale, feeling your chest rise.

Exhale, feeling your chest fall.

For a count of three breaths, allow the mind to do whatever it wants.

Inhale through the nose.

Exhale through the mouth.

Inhale.

Exhale.

Repeat.

On your next inhale, bring your attention back to the body, back to the breath.

Now, bring to mind someone who you have conflict with. Someone who evokes uncomfortable emotions. Someone with whom you are not happy with in this moment.

Remind yourself that just as people only know the parts of you that you choose to show them, so does this person who came to mind.

Imagine this person sitting across from you right now.

See them as human. Someone with a range of emotions who also goes through tough times. Send them some love and kindness by repeating the following:

May you be happy.

May you be healthy.

May you be safe.

May you live with ease.

Continue to follow the breath and when your mind wanderers, let it.

Follow your thoughts as if you are watching ripples on a still lake.

When you are ready, bring your attention back to the sensation of the breath in the body.

Whoever sits before you in your imagination right now, allow them to get up and walk away.

It is just you and your body. You and your breath.

Inhale fully.

Exhale completely

Finish this practice by sending love and kindness into the universe.

May we be happy.

May we be healthy.

May we be safe.

May we live with ease.

*Inspired by Nunez (2020) and Savage (2021).

* * * *

Take time and reflect on your practice at some point before the following day. Write, draw, or think about the emotions and thoughts that came up for you during this practice. How might this practice benefit yourself and others?

_____

_____

_____

_____

_____

_____

Chapter 5: The F-Words

Fight, flight, freeze, fawn—each of these words describe a natural physiological human response to a perceived threat. In any situation that the mind views as dangerous or threatening, the body is triggered to immediately end, decrease, or avoid the threat. This reaction presents itself in one of four ways or a combination of the following:

- Fight: an aggressive response.

- Flight: running away from danger.

- Freeze: unable to move or react to the threat.

- Fawn: acting in a way to please the perpetrator to avoid any further conflict.

Practicing meditation can help you to develop an awareness of your perceptions and control over your reactions. When you can train your attention to notice how you respond in certain situations, you gain a deeper understanding of yourself as well as open the mind to seeking out why you react in this way. Getting to the root of the reaction often enlightens one about another aspect of themselves and the exterior influence that brought on the reaction. This awareness also cultivates feelings of self-compassion and love as you begin to realize that everyone makes mistakes and it is through these that we learn and grow (Frothingham, 2021).

I encourage you to reflect and think about times when you have reacted in the above ways. Which F-word is most common for you? Why might that be? Record your thoughts in the table below or in a personal journal.

F-Words	The Experience	The Feeling(s)	The People Present	The Environment
Fight				
Flight				
Freeze				
Fawn				

Teenage years, while many of the older generations may claim are the best years of your life, those going through it know it is got to get better than this, right? According to the American Academy of Child and Adolescent Psychiatry (2019), every teen experiences at least one of the following stress-inducing experiences:

- changes in their body.

- moving and/or having to change schools.

- living in an unsafe environment or area.

- negative thoughts or feelings about themselves.

- requirements and frustrations from school.

- problems with friends and /or peers.

- difficult family relationships.

- parents getting separated or divorced;

- financial hardship.

- serious illness in themselves, family member, or friend.

- death of a loved one.

- having too many commitments and/or activities.

- unrealistic expectations.

Teens feeling overwhelmed by stress are at risk for developing anxiety, physical illness, poor coping skills such as alcohol or drugs, aggression, or withdraw and self-isolation. There are many healthy ways you can manage stress including but not limited to a balanced diet, an appropriate amount of sleep (13-19 year-old require a minimum of 8-10 hours), exercise and time spent in nature, a close group of trusted friends, and a mindfulness and meditation routine. When you find it difficult to show yourself love, surround yourself with people who will show you their love and support (Frothingham, 2021).

The following meditations are often used to help reduce stress and negative thinking, to improve quality of mental health, soften any tension and increase self-love. I invite you to practice both meditations at some point, stressed or not, and notice how your outlook changes. Notice how your body reacts to the breath practice and reflect on the feelings that come up. Find times throughout your day to add some of the techniques you have acquired thus far in efforts to build the muscles of the mind.

Set a timer or sound a bell to commence and complete each practice should you enjoy it. The meditations can be shortened or lengthened to suit your schedule.

Mindfulness: Breathing Meditation (Five Minutes)

Get into a comfortable position and settle into this space.

Allow the body to feel heavy. Notice the weight and connection between your body and the surface.

Without trying to change or control the breath, bring your awareness to it.

Feel the temperature of the air as it passes through your nostrils with each inhale and exhale.

Feel the body and breath move together as one. Notice the body rises as it fills and falls as it empties.

If you struggle to focus on your breath at this moment, take some time to allow your mind to wander.

Notice the thoughts that arise. Do not judge the thought or yourself.

Thoughts are natural. They occur for everyone. Follow your thoughts as they go through the mind like leaves blowing in a gentle breeze.

When ready, gently guide your attention back to the breath. Back to the sensation of the breath coming into and leaving the body.

Keeping your attention on the breath, inhale through the nose.

Breathing in, I know I am breathing in.

Exhale through the mouth.

Breathing out, I know I am breathing out.

Repeating these phrases of awareness keeps your mind in the present moment.

Inhale.

Breathing in, I know I am breathing in.

Exhale.

Breathing out, I know I am breathing out.

Try to keep this focus for five breaths.

Inhale fully.

Exhale completely.

When the mind wanders, notice, and gently bring your awareness back to the breath.

Breathing in, I feel my body fill with life.

Breathing out, I feel my body relax.

If you notice sounds, emotions, tensions, acknowledge them but do not explain, justify, or judge them. Just breathe and allow these things to wash over you.

Inhale fully.

Exhale completely.

I breathe in this moment.

I know this is a special moment.

I inhale peace, 1, 2, 3.

I exhale joy, 1, 2, 3.

Continue to follow the breath for the remainder of this practice.

Notice how your mind and body have changed since before the practice.

It is normal for the mind to wander. The goal is not to empty the mind, but to train your attention like a muscle you would train at the gym.

-Inspired by Celestine (2020).

* * * *

It has been suggested by Buddhist Monk, Tich Nhat Hanh that one can easily incorporate mindful breathing into their day by choosing reminders or triggers for the mind to tune into the breath. For example, every time you open a door, focus your attention on your breath. If you stop at a red light, focus on your breath until the light turns green. The more often you tune into the breath, the more able you will be able to cope with stress as it comes up. Your breath is always with you; your mind is not. It is natural for the mind to live in the past or in the future, and takes training to stay in the present. Practice makes improvement; keep going.

Relaxation: Guided Imagery

The purpose of guided imagery is for you to be able to transport yourself to a place of calm and peace. Using your five senses, you can send positive comforting messages to the mind, body that reduce feelings of anxiety and help ease psychological and physical distress or pain (Nguyen & Brymer, 2018).

As for all meditation practices, it takes time to train attention. It is completely normal for the mind to wander during a guided imagery practice, so when this happens, notice it and gently refocus your attention on one of the five senses. The more you practice, the easier the technique will become, so don't be hard on yourself if this is difficult at first. This is your practice and no one else's. Take all the time you need.

Guided imagery relaxation is better practiced lying down in a comfortable position where you are unlikely to be interrupted. A quiet space is ideal and, if possible, play soft sounds of the place you'd like to imagine. While this meditation is a walk through the forest, you can find many others out there that suit the space you feel most comfortable and relaxed.

Mindfulness: Walking Through the Woods (Eleven Minutes)

Get into a comfortable position, lying on your back if possible, and cover yourself with a blanket if you like.

Allow your body to begin to relax. The feet turned out, arms resting at your sides, palms facing up, fingers naturally curled. Eyes softly closed.

Full inhale through the nose.

I relax my body.

Sigh, exhale through the mouth

My body is relaxed.

Inhale, *I relax my body.*

Exhale, my *body is relaxed.*

Inhale, 1, 2, 3, 4, 5.

Notice the shift to Exhale, 1, 2, 3, 4, 5

Resume your natural rhythm of breath.

Imagine you are standing at the edge of a field, looking out toward a tree line of various shades of greens, browns and yellows.

The softly blows warm air around you, gently rustling the leaves in the trees up ahead.

You take your first step into the field.

Feel the firm support of the ground you walk on.

You lift your arms slightly as you walk through the field, toward the woods, allowing the wheat to tickle your arms.

The sun shines brightly, covering the field in a golden blanket.

You approach the edge of the woods and set foot on the path leading inside.

The light of the sun cascades through the canopy highlighting the textures and colors of the forest.

Up above you, the blue from the sky peaks through all the spaces and crevices of the leaves.

Strong, towering brown tree trunks surround you, colorful bushes, and small sprouts all reaching up toward the light.

Snuggled in around the bottoms of trees is velvety moss, soft to the touch.

You feel the ground's slight shift as it holds each step you take.

Inhale and notice the smell of the pine trees, of the moss, of the summery air.

Exhale and relax into each step as the earth parts slightly to cradle your feet.

Inhale and allow the body to relax.

Exhale, filling the forest with your breath of life.

As you walk, you begin to tune into the chirping sounds of birds and the small squeaks of squirrels.

You hear the babbling of a brook up ahead and walk toward the flowing water.

The path you walk upon is strewn with fallen leaves and patches of moss. Pinecones and acorns scatter the wood floor. Roots roll over the ground like clouds over a hill.

As you approach the stream, you find a spot to sit.

The forest floor feels soft underneath you. The ground is cool, and the air is warm.

You notice the textures and colors of the bark on the trees that encircle you. Some of it is rough, some smooth, some peeling back, revealing new layers. Some tree bark is light while others are dark.

The gentle sound of rocks rolling in the moving water pulls your attention back to the stream. You remove your shoes and socks and dip your toes into the water, testing the temperature before submerging your feet.

The water is cool and smooth, changing its shape and running its course around your feet, between your toes and you watch as it swirls and pours downstream.

Your focus on the water grows, you begin to notice the rhythmic sound of running water.

With each breath, your body relaxes further, the woods hugging you as if exist in nature.

The sound of a woodpecker in search of food brings your attention back to your feet. You decide it's time to leave and take your feet out of the water, noticing the polite sounding drips that flow back into the stream as you dry shake your feet dry.

Putting your shoes back on, you take in the familiar sights, smells, and sounds of the woods. You use the stream water to cool your hands, placing them on your face. The cool water soothes your warm sun-kissed skin. Feeling droplets on your lips, you lick the cool refreshing water and feel prepared for the journey home.

As you walk, you notice the different sounds of the forest. The birds, squirrels, and rustling leaves. The crunch of the ground as you walk, the distant sound of the water running as you approach the path's exit.

Before leaving, you turn and take in the woods.

Inhale through the nose, taking in the pleasant aroma of nature.

Exhale through the mouth, offering gratitude to the woods for carrying you along your journey.

You turn toward the field, knowing you can return to this peaceful place any time.

Walk out into the field of sunshine, feel the warmth of the sun on your face, open your eyes, return to your body, and return to your awareness.

-Inspired by Flannery (2022).

* * * *

I encourage you to imagine a place that brings you peace, love, and safety. You can create your own guided imagery relaxation by building this place in your mind via the five senses. Think about the colors, sounds, textures, emotions, tastes, and anything that can connect the mind to the environment of choice. Take time to imagine this place, draw it in a sketchbook, or describe it in a journal. No matter how you choose to reflect, do so knowing that this is your safe space and no one else's. You are in control. You have the power to overcome obstacles and meditation is one tool that is readily available for you.

Record your ideas below or in a personal journal.

Senses	My Spot
Feels like	
Sounds like	

Smells like	
Tastes like	
Looks like	
Helps me to feel	

Chapter 6: Self-Discovery

"Three things cannot hide for long: the Moon, the Sun, and the Truth"
—Buddha

During teenage years you are discovering who you are while also trying to navigate so many other factors that can be overwhelming. Sometimes self-love takes a back seat as you might choose to try to fit in rather than to find where you belong. You may pretend to like something you do not actually like to fit in with people you want to be friends with or to get someone to like you. You might alter your voice, wardrobe, and interests to fit in where you think you'll be happy, but eventually, this will become too much. You cannot hide your true self and live and happy life at the same time.

Self-discovery is something you are always learning as you go through life trying new things, having various experiences, building and fostering relationships, experiencing loss, etc. Do not shy away from opportunity, and do not allow fear to control your destiny. Build your self-love and embrace the unknown; learn more about yourself by living life openly rather than closed off.

Finding where you belong means following your heart, doing what makes you happy, and what makes you feel like yourself. When you embrace this, you will find people who support you unconditionally. You will feel like you belong when you find a space where people welcome you with open arms. Mindfulness, Self-love, and Meditation can help you own your uniqueness, can help you tune into your true self, and empower you to follow your heart with confidence.

Keep a journal nearby to record any thoughts that may come up during the following meditations.

Meditation: Mirror Work / Self-Discovery (Five Minutes)

Choosing a well-lit space, free from distraction or interruption, stand or sit in front of a mirror that allows you to see your reflection clearly.

Take a few deep, relaxing breaths as you scan your body, appreciating how it bends, folds and curves on your way up to noticing your face.

Inhale fully.

Exhale completely.

The only goal of this meditation is to be here now, with yourself, resisting any judgmental voice that may try to creep in.

You can begin this meditation with your eyes closed. Simply breathe and tune into your body.

Notice how the body moves and flows with the breath.

Notice the temperature of the breath as it enters and exits the body.

Inhale, 1, 2, 3.

Hold, 1, 2, 3.

Exhale, 3, 2, 1.

Hold, 1, 2, 3.

Repeat three times before resuming your natural rhythm of breath.

Inhale, *I am loved.*

Exhale, *I am safe.*

Inhale, *I deserve to be happy.*

Exhale, *I choose to do what brings me joy.*

Breathe.

When you are ready, gently open your eyes and begin to gaze at your reflection.

Notice the curvature of your face, the angles of your cheekbones, the shape and color of your eyes, and the slight arch in the eyebrows.

Take in your face. Hold yourself with grace and breathe.

Notice how the breath has changed since opening your eyes. Is it slower or faster? Deeper or shallower?

Inhale, my *body is powerful.*

Exhale, *I know what I need.*

Inhale, *I see the world with my eyes.*

Exhale, *I feel the world with my heart.*

Gaze into your eyes. Notice the shape and color of your eyes.

What do you see when you look in the mirror?

What feelings come up for you as you take in your image?

Breathe.

If you notice your inner critique begin to rise, refocus your attention by counting the breath.

1. Inhale through the nose. Exhale through the mouth.

2. Inhale through the nose. Exhale through the mouth.

3. Inhale through the nose. Exhale through the mouth.

If the critique is too loud, notice that. Bring your attention to what happens within the body when this voice is present.

Keeping your gaze on your reflection, begin to see yourself as a child.

Look into young eyes and offer them some kindness.

Breathe as you remember what carefree felt like. The carefree joy of being a child, too young to have been jaded by difficult experiences or events. The warm, happiness that is in that child is in you too.

Breathe.

Inhale, *I am here for you.*

Exhale, *you have permission to be yourself.*

Complete this practice whenever feels natural for you.

-Inspired by Well (2020).

* * * *

In a personal journal or reflecting before moving on with your day, think about the practice you have just completed. When was the last time you looked in the mirror and really looked into your eyes with love? Take time to record your thoughts using the prompts below if you like.

How did this practice make you feel from beginning to end?

_____

_____

_____

_____

_____

_____

What was your initial reaction to looking in the mirror?

_____

_____

_____

_____

_____

What thoughts or feelings stand out the most for you in this moment?

_____

_____

_____

_____

_____

_____

_____

Whose voice did you hear? Was it your own or someone else's?

_____

_____

_____

_____

_____

Comment on the quality of your thoughts throughout this practice.

_____

_____

_____

_____

_____

Mirror work can help you to discover more self-confidence, self-compassion, and self-acceptance. The more you see yourself for who you are, the more you will lean into your desires, joys and voices. Seek opportunities for self-discovery and grow into you, grow into a state of self-acceptance.

Mindfulness: Movement (Fifteen minutes)

This practice aims to connect body, breath, and mind in order to help you gain self-awareness, move with intention, and be mindful of the present moment. As we go through this meditation practice, pay curious attention to the way the body feels with each movement. Notice any messages the body sends to you and honor those messages.

This movement practice is not meant to cause pain, strain or uncomfortable sensations. If you notice stress or tension building, bring your attention to this area and breathe. If you feel a pose is uncomfortable or inaccessible for you, breathe and adjust your body until you find a place of comfort.

Before practicing mindful movement, be aware of any personal or physical limitations and position yourself in a way that allows you to move safely. Breathe deeply, in and out, visualizing softness and space coming into the body.

This is not a workout for the body, but for the mind. It should not feel forced.

With this in mind, come into a standing position.

Stand with a tall spine, as if a string is pulling your head up like that of a marionette.

Plant your feet into the floor by pressing through the heels.

Wiggle your toes until you can comfortably hold them against the floor, feeling the connection between ground and body.

Breathing in, filling the body.

Breathing out, emptying the body.

Breathing in, *I know I am breathing in.*

Breathing out, *I know I am breathing out.*

Remaining in the standing pose, allow your shoulders to roll forward and up on the inhale, and back and down on the exhale.

Notice any sensations in your shoulders as you roll them forward and back and up and down. Continue breathing with a natural rhythm as you move mindfully.

Inhale, *I am aware that I am rolling my shoulders forward.*

Exhale, *I am aware that I am rolling my shoulders backward.*

71

Reserve the shoulder roll until you have completed equal rolls both forward and back.

On your next exhale, release the shoulders and allow them to relax, coming back to a neutral position.

Inhale through the nose.

Exhale through the mouth.

Next, roll your neck forward and down, facing the floor.

Inhale, gently rolling the neck to the right, with your ear close to or touching your right shoulder.

Exhale, rolling the neck forward and down.

Inhale, gently rolling the neck to the left, with your ear close to or touching your left shoulder.

Exhale, rolling the neck forward and down.

Breathing in and out, roll the neck gently to each side three times before slowly raising your head, and coming back to a neutral position.

Check in with your body as you breathe and notice any areas of tension or stress. Visualize your breath going there, releasing any pain or discomfort.

With the next inhale, bring your arms up above your head, palms facing each other.

On the exhale, bring your arms down and allow your palms to meet in front of your heart.

Inhale, arms rise.

Exhale, arms fall.

Continue this practice of raising and lowering the arms with the movement of the breath. Going along at your own pace; not too fast.

Breathe in as your arms rise.

Breathe out and let your arms come down.

Repeat this breath and body motion for the count of five inhales and five exhales.

When you are ready, come back to your standing pose, arms relaxed at your sides. Still, strong, and grounded like a mountain.

Inhale fully.

Exhale completely.

Inhale, raise your arms above your head.

Exhale, lower your arms, and fold at the waist.

Bend your knees slightly and allow your top half to hang. Arms and head hanging effortlessly like a rag doll.

Find length in your spine, ensuring that you are bending more at the waist instead of the back.

Breathe.

Notice any sensations in the body as you bend forward.

Breathe for three more cycles.

After the final exhale, place your hands on your hips.

Gently and slowly rise on the inhale. Straightening the waist without any rush.

Stand and breathe.

Notice how you feel at this moment.

Inhale fully.

Exhale completely.

Softly come down to a seated position with your legs out in front of you, a slight bend in the knee, or perhaps, in a chair with the feet firmly planted on the floor.

Inhale and lengthen the body.

Exhale and fold over your legs.

Inhale.

Exhale, reaching toward your feet.

Inhale, notice and sensations in your legs, hips, and spine.

Exhale, and feel the body relax.

After two or three breaths, allow your body to rise on the next inhale, coming back to a comfortable seated position.

Exhale, releasing any tension.

For our last movement, we will twist. First, place your right hand on your left hip and the left hand on your lower back.

Inhale to sit up tall.

Exhale to twist, looking over the left shoulder.

Inhale, find length in the spine.

Exhale, twist.

Breathing in and out for a count of three before coming back to neutral on the last exhale.

Inhale fully.

Exhale completely.

Now, place your left hand on your right hip and the other on your lower back.

Inhale, finding length in the spine.

Exhale, twisting to the right, looking over the right shoulder.

Breathing in, *I know that I am twisting.*

Breathing out, *I smile.*

Count three complete breath cycles, noticing any sensations in the body.

Exhale, slowly returning to a neutral seated posture facing forward.

Place one hand over your heart and the other over your belly.

Breathe.

Inhale, *I am aware of my body.*

Exhale, *I smile at my body with awareness and compassion.*

-Inspired by Dzung X. Vo (n.d.).

* * * *

Before jumping back into your life beyond this mindful movement practice, take some time to reflect.

How did you feel throughout the practice?

_____

_____

_____

_____

_____

_____

What sensations or thoughts came up for you?

_____

_____

_____

_____

_____

_____

Conclusion

It is with magnificent pleasure and gratitude that I welcome you to the close of this book. I hope within these pages that you have found pieces of yourself once lost, aspects you never knew existed, come out with a new-found love and confidence in yourself. Introducing and continuing Mindfulness, Self-love, And Meditation practice into your daily routine will have immeasurable positive impacts on your mental, physical and emotional health. Come back to the practices within this book anytime you need guidance and reassurance that yes, life is be hard, but you can get through it. You can train your mind to notice the good times and find light in the darkness.

The benefits of mindfulness self-compassion are limitless. When you decide that you are important enough, worthy enough, deserving enough of love and kindness, you will begin to see the world through a whole new lens. This book was about helping you to accept yourself as you are, to embrace every aspect that makes you. No one in this world is immune to challenges or setbacks, so go forward in life holding your head high, knowing that you are not alone, knowing that we are all navigating this life as best we can.

As your mind and body continue to grow and change, find comfort in the fact that the changes within the body happen to everyone at different rates and in different ways. When you experience intense emotions or are faced with challenges, remind yourself that you have everything you need to get through this moment. Know that the range of human emotions is vast and universal, and that everyone struggles with themselves at one point or another throughout their life. Meditation is a practice to incorporate, not a goal to attain and move on from.

Training the mind's attention takes time, so be gentle with yourself. The more you are able to tune into and notice the quality of your thoughts, the easier it will be to gain control over your inner dialogue and outer reactions and responses to various stimuli. By accepting what is, we can gain inner peace. This is not to be confused with accepting inappropriate, disrespectful, or harmful behavior, actions, or words. Accepting situations for how they are and being mindful of your emotions can guide you to choose a path that will help you thrive rather than a path that will keep you down.

I encourage you to continue exploring meditation practices to enhance your understanding of self, to increase empathy and compassion for others, and learn more about what it means to live a happy fulfilling life just as you are.

"I don't think that loving yourself is a choice. I think that it's a decision that has to be made for survival" —Lizzo

Thank you so much for supporting my dream as an independent author. Your decision to purchase and read my book means everything to me! I couldn't have made it this far without amazing readers like you!

As you know, reviews are crucial for independent authors like me to reach a wider audience and continue pursuing our passion.

I would greatly appreciate it if you could leave an honest review on Amazon by scanning the QR code below or going to the link below.

obiez.com/reviewmeditation

References

American Academy of Child and Adolescent Psychiatry. (2019, January). *Stress Management and Teens.* Aacap.org; American Academy of Child and Adolescent Psychiatry. https://www.aacap.org/aacap/families_and_youth/fac ts_for_families/fff-guide/helping-teenagers-with-stress-066.aspx

Amir-Yaffe, G. (2021, March 5). *10 Cool Meditations for Pre-Teens and Teens.* DOYOU.COM; DOYOU Media Pte. Ltd. https://www.doyou.com/10-cool-meditations-for-pre-teens-and-teens-67578/

Celestine, N. (2020, August 15). *What is Mindful Breathing? Exercises, Scripts and Videos.* PositivePsychology.com. https://positivepsychology.com/mindful-breathing/

Creswell, J. D., & Khoury, B. (2019, October 30). *Mindfulness Meditation: A research-proven way to reduce stress.* Apa.org. https://www.apa.org/topics/mindfulness/meditation #:~:text=What%20is%20mindfulness%20meditation %3F

EveryDayPower. (2020, January 4). *50 Lizzo Quotes to Encourage You to Love Yourself More*. Everyday Power. https://everydaypower.com/lizzo-quotes/

Fargo, S. (2020, September 24). *Cultivating Joy*. Mindfulness Exercises. https://mindfulnessexercises.com/cultivating-joy/

Flannery, B. (2022). *Guided Imagery Forest Path Script for Relaxation -by Blake Flannery Why Imagine a Forest for Relaxation?* In *Remedy Grove*. https://irp-cdn.multiscreensite.com/d6355722/files/uploaded/Guided%20Imagery%20Forest%20Path%20Script%20for%20Relaxation%20May%202024%202020.pdf

Frothingham, M. B. (2021, October 6). *Fight, Flight, Freeze, or Fawn: How We Respond to Threats - Simply Psychology*. Www.simplypsychology.org. https://www.simplypsychology.org/fight-flight-freeze-fawn.html

Gelles, D. (2019). How to Meditate. *The New York Times*. https://www.nytimes.com/guides/well/how-to-meditate

Gratitude Meditation Script. (n.d.). In *Change to Chill*. Retrieved February 11, 2023, from https://www.changetochill.org/wp-content/uploads/2018/08/Gratitude-Meditation-Script-1.pdf

GreatMeditation. (2021, October 11). *I am Thankful Guided Meditation for Gratitude.* Www.youtube.com; Great Meditation. https://www.youtube.com/watch?v=bi0qUKHLbX8

Milne, A. (2019, October 4). *10 Health and Well-being Perks of Journaling for Teenagers.* #Slowchathealth. https://slowchathealth.com/2019/10/04/journaling-perks/

Moore, M. (2022, July 26). *Mindful Self-Compassion: 4 Practices to Try.* Psych Central. https://psychcentral.com/blog/the-practice-of-self-compassion-and-reducing-stress#next-steps

Nguyen, J., & Brymer, E. (2018). *Nature-Based Guided Imagery as an Intervention for State Anxiety.* Frontiers in Psychology, *9*(1858). https://doi.org/10.3389/fpsyg.2018.01858

Nunez, K. (2020, June 9). *Metta Meditation: 5 Benefits and Tips for Beginners.* Healthline. https://www.healthline.com/health/metta-meditation#how-to

Robledo, I. (2021, April 18). *Guide To Mindful Eating For Kids» Making Mindfulness Fun.* Making Mindfulness Fun. https://www.makingmindfulnessfun.com/mindful-eating-for-kids/

Savage, J. (2021, June 23). *A loving kindness meditation script - and 7 reasons to use it!* Ekhart Yoga. https://www.ekhartyoga.com/articles/meditation/loving-kindness-meditation-script-and-7-reasons-to-use-it

Schultz, J. (2020, July 24). *5 Differences Between Mindfulness and Meditation.* PositivePsychology.com. https://positivepsychology.com/differences-between-mindfulness-meditation/#differences

Selva, J. (2017, June 18). *76 Most Powerful Mindfulness Quotes: Your Daily Dose of Inspiration.* PositivePsychology.com. https://positivepsychology.com/mindfulness-quotes/

Suri, K. (2019, February 17). *BKS Iyengar Quotes – 100 Inspirational and Motivational Quotes by B.K.S Iyengar.* The Yogi Press. https://www.yogi.press/home/bks-iyengar-quotes

Vo, D. X. (n.d.). *MINDFUL MOVEMENT FOR TEENS.* https://ggie.berkeley.edu/wp-content/uploads/2020/04/GGIE_Mindful_Movement_for_Teens.pdf

Well, T. (2020, January 2). *What the Mirror Can Teach You About Yourself: Advice from a Mirror Gazing Expert.* Mindful. https://www.mindful.org/what-the-mirror-can-teach-you-about-yourself-advice-from-a-mirror-gazing-expert/